F̶.̶.̶.̶ ll
available for limited time

Hi Spirituality Lovers!

My name is Silvia Hill, and first off, I want to THANK YOU for reading my book.

Now you have a chance to join my exclusive spirituality email list so you can get the ebooks below for free as well as the potential to get more spirituality ebooks for free! Simply click the link below to join.

P.S. Remember that it's 100% free to join the list.

~~$27~~ FREE BONUSES

- 🙌 9 Types of Spirit Guides and How to Connect to Them
- 🙌 How to Develop Your Intuition: 7 Secrets for Psychic Development and Tarot Reading
- 🙌 Tarot Reading Secrets for Love, Career, and General Messages

Access your free bonuses here
https://livetolearn.lpages.co/silvia-astrology-for-beginners/

Contents

Astrology for Beginners

A Simple Guide to the Twelve Zodiac Signs, Planets, Birth Charts, and Astrological Divination

Introduction

When was the last time somebody asked you what your zodiac sign was? For many people, this question is as important as learning where someone grew up or what they do for a living. It provides the opportunity to learn things about others that they may not even know themselves.

Your zodiac sign can reveal a great deal about you, which is why we are always curious to learn about other people's signs. It is like a manual that gives insight into ourselves and the people in our lives. That being said, astrology provides more than just personality traits and horoscopes.

Astrology shows you are a part of this vast universe. Its countless secrets and wonders are hidden in the stars, waiting to be revealed. Learning about your zodiac sign and birth chart will help guide you through your life's journey, providing you with direction and purpose for every aspect of your life, including your relationships and career. A birth chart shows the planets' position on the day and hour you were born and serves to help you understand various aspects of your personality and character traits, but also your aspirations and a specific trajectory for your lifetime.

Let's be honest: Astrology can be overwhelming for absolute novices who don't know the first thing about signs, houses, or charts. For this reason, we have designed this book to be simple and accessible, so it can serve as a basic guide to introduce you to this vast topic. You will find all the information you are seeking at this stage of your learning, including instructions, hands-on methods, and answers to many questions you may have about the study and practice of astrology.

Throughout these pages, you will find information and interesting facts about zodiac signs to improve your understanding and complete your knowledge of astrology. After reading this book, you will grasp all the basics of astrology and be able to have conversations with your friends about your new favorite topic.

Take the journey now, and immerse yourself in the fascinating world of astrology. Get ready to learn about who you are, your hidden potential, and how to find out what the stars and planets have in store for you.

Chapter 1: Astrology 101

Suppose you've always been fascinated by star signs or horoscopes. In that case, it's a good indication that you're interested in the world of astrology. But what is astrology? Is it simply limited to horoscopes based on your birth date, or is it something more?

While this book will cover everything you need to know about the zodiac, birth charts, and astrological divination, you should first understand what astrology actually is. This opening chapter will provide useful historical context and introduce you to the concepts of astrology in their most basic sense.

Astrology 101

The dictionary's definition of astrology is "the study of the movements and positions of the sun, moon, planets, and stars in the belief that they affect the character and lives of people." Unlike astronomy, it isn't an exact science. Instead, it involves making observations about the positions of celestial objects like stars and planets to make predictions about people's lives and events on earth.

Astrology is a popular pastime today, but it has a long history. In fact, its origins date back to Mesopotamia in the 3rd millennium BC, and for a while, it was considered the same as astronomy.

From Mesopotamia, astrology spread to India, but it was in Egypt and Greece that it truly developed. In 525 BC, Egypt was conquered by the Persians 525, who introduced them to astrology. When the country was occupied by Alexander the Great in 332 BC, the Egyptians introduced the Greeks to this subject.

In Ptolemaic Egypt, Mesopotamian and Babylonian astrology were combined with Egyptian astrology to form the first horoscopic astrology. The horoscopes used by the Egyptians greatly differ from what we use today but formed the basis on which today's astrology is dependent.

In parallel, the Greeks in Greece were making use of new astrological concepts, including horoscopes. Another type of astrology developed by the Greeks was theurgic astrology, which used astrology to help a person's soul reach the gods.

Following the Roman conquest of Greece, astrology was initially treated as a subject for the lower orders of society. However, this did not last long, and soon enough, Roman emperors brought in court astrologers, starting with the emperor, Tiberius. At this point, astrology was still indistinguishable from astronomy, and astrologer Claudius Ptolemy made the first attempt at creating an accurate world map. Ptolemy wanted to use it to understand the relationship between where a person was born and the heavenly bodies visible in the area. He also coined the term "geography," the study of the earth (from the Greek *geo*, meaning earth, and *graphia*, meaning writing).

Astrology was also extremely popular in the Islamic world at that time, especially after the fall of the Mediterranean city of Alexandria to the Arabs. Several works by Islamic astrologers would later become popular in medieval Europe.

However, this was also the first time astrology and astronomy were differentiated. Astronomers claimed astrologers were making their judgments based on conjectural grounds (observation and interpretation) rather than empirical grounds (factual and scientific) as supported by astronomy.

In the Western world, astronomy was relegated to a second-rank discipline due to the breakup of the Greek and Roman empires. However, Arab and Muslim astrological works were translated into Latin and made their way to Europe starting from the 10th century, leading to a resurgence in popularity.

At the end of the 12th century, astrology became more integrated into the lives of Europeans. Astrology helped not only in guiding regular people – but professionals too. Doctors consulted with the stars when they were treating illnesses and ailments. It even became a requirement sometime in the 16th century for doctors to calculate the moon's position before performing more serious procedures on patients.

Astrology was also incorporated into other parts of daily life, including literature and university education. However, by the end of the Renaissance, the popularity of astronomy plummeted. By the end of the 18th century, there was little scientific interest in it.

Nowadays, the popularity of astrology varies in different parts of the world. In India, for example, it is still a major part of daily life and has retained its importance in society. By contrast, astrology is less part of the scientific canon in the West, but that doesn't mean there is no popular interest in it. It even gained a strong following in the 1960s. Astrology in the West largely revolves around the 12 zodiac signs, and most popular horoscopes are designed around them.

The Zodiac Signs

As you're aware, there are 12 zodiac signs in Western astrology. These are based on the Earth's 360-degree orbit around the sun, with each 30-degree section making up one full zodiac sign. The signs are also associated with different periods of the year, seasons, signs, and celestial rulers. We'll be going into more details on these later in the book.

There are four main branches of modern astrology:

- **Natal Astrology:** A birth chart can be created by combining the person's place, time, and date of birth. This chart can then be used to sketch a portrait of their personality and what journey their lives will take.

- **Mundane Astrology:** Unlike natal astrology, mundane astrology doesn't focus on individuals but on the world as a whole and countries and governments in particular. This branch of astrology uses astrological concepts to predict how international political and financial systems will turn out, and some believe it can also be used to predict natural disasters. It's thought to be the oldest branch of astrology.

- **Electional Astrology:** This branch uses astrology to determine the right time to start a new business or another major undertaking. It considers both the people involved and the place where the action will take place.

- **Horary Astrology:** When looking for specific answers to a question, you can use the time and place to guide you. Where and when was the question asked? Use this data to form your horary chart.

Of course, there are other branches of astrology as well, depending on what a person is looking for; these include medical astrology, financial astrology, and relationship astrology.

Birth Charts

Another notorious aspect of astrology is the practice of making birth charts. Your birth chart takes the position of celestial bodies at the time of your birth to create a chart for your past, present, and future.

The locations of these celestial bodies matter because each serves a different purpose in your birth chart. Your chart is divided into inner planets, which are the planets and bodies with short orbits (the sun, moon, and Mercury), and the outer planets, which are the remaining celestial bodies. In a nutshell, the inner planets impact your day-to-day experiences and help shape your personality, whereas the outer planets impact the larger themes in your life, as well as how your ancestors influence your life.

Your natal or birth chart is divided into 12 sections, known as houses. Each house represents a singular aspect of your life, such as personal finances, career, love matters, philosophy, and psychic abilities. How the outer planets impact the larger arc of your life depends on which houses they are placed in – the houses and the planets that inhabit them help display your strengths and weaknesses.

The interpretation of a birth chart rests upon three pillars:

- The planet you're referencing
- The zodiac sign that rules
- The house that planet is in

Based on these three elements, you will be able to understand your personality and that of others better.

Another important aspect of your birth chart is your rising sign. When you are born, look to the East. There, you will find your zodiac sign, the sign that was rising at the moment of your conception. When you plot your birth chart, your rising sign will play a large role in how you fit into the world.

If you're hoping to learn more about your birth chart and how to analyze it, you're in luck, as that will be covered in an upcoming chapter.

Horoscopes

Horoscopes are similar to natal charts in that they involve creating a chart of the heavens at a specific moment in time. Now, while a natal chart reflects the specific moment of an individual's birth, a horoscope can be a chart of any moment in time. This horoscope is then used as a predictive tool, like a natal chart, to help predict what will happen in the future.

The Practice of Astrology

In the past, practicing astrology was a complex endeavor that required a detailed understanding of how the celestial world worked. However, today, doing so is relatively easier. For example, you can learn how to create your natal chart online, and some online tools will even do the job for you.

Once you have your natal chart (or any other horoscope) ready, the next step is to learn how to interpret it, which this book was designed to help you do. That said, you should get the basics down first, and that begins with understanding how the planets (and other celestial bodies) are used in modern astrology. To learn more, proceed to the next chapter. Once you understand the importance of the planets, you'll also learn how to analyze your natal chart, discover why your zodiac sign is important, and learn how to use your natal chart to make fairly accurate predictions.

Chapter 2: Identifying the Planets

Planets, specifically their symbolism and movement across space, play a central role in modern astrology. Planets, stars, and human beings are matter, made of atoms and all sorts of physical and chemical reactions. As a result of the similarities we share with the universe, we naturally react to its various cycles. We are one with the cosmos, which is why the movements of the planets can greatly impact our health, feelings, thoughts, and actions. Each planet and its position influence our personality, help us predict our future, and teaches us about the zodiac signs we are most compatible with. Simply put, they serve as guides to help us better understand our physical and spiritual selves.

Planets are different, with each symbolizing certain traits and qualities of our personalities and influencing one or more zodiac signs. After learning what each planet means in astrology, you will understand how their positioning and movements can give you insight into your personality and help you predict your future. However, the Earth isn't one of these planets because it is our home, and its position in space has strictly no impact on our lives.

Types of Planets in Astrology

To begin on a solid basis, there are two types of planets to distinguish between in astrology: "inner" planets, which are also called "personal" planets, and "outer" planets, usually referred to as "generational" planets.

The Inner/Personal Planets

The inner planets consist of the Sun, the Moon, Mercury, Venus, and Mars. It may surprise you to see the Moon and the Sun referred to as planets since this contradicts what we have learned in elementary science class. However, astrology applies its own meaning and interpretation of celestial bodies in how to identify them. For instance, astrologists don't consider the Sun to be a star, but they regard it, along with the Moon, as planets known as "luminaries."

These planets have the biggest impact on our daily life, including our relationships, emotions, certain events, and how we interact with other people. This is because personal planets lie inside the Earth's orbit and can travel from one zodiac sign to another at a faster pace than outer planets, which is how they can directly influence our day-to-day lives.

The Outer/Generational Planets

The outer planets consist of Jupiter, Saturn, Uranus, Neptune, and Pluto. Although contemporary astronomers have identified Pluto as a "dwarf planet," astrologers still consider it a planet in its own right and characteristics. These planets are further from the Earth and move through zodiacs at a slower pace than the inner planet's counterparts, which is why they affect our lives differently. It can take generational planets anywhere from 18 months to over a decade to move from one zodiac sign to another.

For this reason, gauging their true impact on our daily lives can be a lot more difficult because during these years, we can go through many changes as a result of our experiences of growing up. So, it can be tricky to determine whether it was time or the planet's position that did influence our personality. That said, outer planets can influence your circumstances and bigger events that can impact many people's lives collectively, not just from an individual standpoint.

Now, let's discuss each planet and its role in astrology.

The Sun

Glyph: ☉

In astrology, the sun's glyph (or symbol) is a circle with a dot in the middle. This symbol has a deeper meaning: the circle represents life while the dot is the sun, the center of everything, including who we are.

Positive Side

The sun's strong presence in your zodiac sign makes you full of life and pushes you to figure out your dreams and make them a reality. It also makes you warm, happy, confident, dignified, and creative, allowing your personality to shine through and come up with unique ideas. Additionally, the sun will make you "shine" and particularly excel in leadership positions. Your health and well-being also improve thanks to the sun's presence.

Negative Side

The sun has a negative side as well. At times, when it is strongly present in your zodiac sign, it can negatively impact your personality and make you arrogant, judgmental, egocentric, and even lethargic. By contrast, when its presence is weak, it can cause various health problems like cardiovascular issues, headaches, poor eyesight, baldness, affect your bones' health, and impact your blood circulation.

Meaning

The sun isn't only the center of the universe. It is the center of our being as well. It represents our rational side, experiences, ego, purpose, identity, life force, and reason. No other planet in astrology has a bigger influence on your personality and existence in general than the mighty sun.

The Moon

Glyph: ☽

The glyph of the moon is a crescent shape. It doesn't look like a full moon because it represents our emotions and the struggle and emptiness we feel as a result of the many contradictions we bear inside of us.

Positive Side

Suppose you have the moon in your zodiac sign. In that case, you are more likely to have a lively imagination, be creative, adapt well to new situations, and be intuitive.

Negative Side

The moon in your zodiac can leave you prone to moodiness and restlessness.

Meaning

The moon represents our emotions and deepest, most private, and most vulnerable selves that we usually hide deep inside and only share with those we trust. It represents your nurturing side and is connected to feminine energies, feelings of security, family, and the home. It also governs our unconscious.

Mercury

Glyph: ☿

The cross on the bottom of Mercury's glyph symbolizes how the planet helps you manifest your inner self to the world, while the half-circle showcases Mercury's ability to push you into reaching your "higher self" (the conscious, eternal, most achieved version of ourselves).

Positive Side

Mercury helps you stay curious, versatile, clever, and inquisitive, improving your communication skills. It also provides us with the analytical and intellectual skills to understand life's most riddling contradictions. This planet symbolizes the rational side of our personality and governs how we communicate with the world around us. It also impacts how we process and share thoughts and information and how we solve our problems. For that reason, it is also associated with our time-management and organizational skills.

Negative Side

Mercury can make you overly technical, indecisive, and nervous. When this planet retrogrades (when a planet appears to be moving backward from our earthly perspective), it can cause travel delays, communication issues, and unwanted solicitations from ex-partners.

Meaning

In mythology, Mercury was the Roman God of finance and commerce and a messenger of the gods. As the smallest planet in the solar system, Mercury is named after this deity. It strongly impacts our personalities and lives due to its close proximity to our own home planet.

Venus

Glyph: ♀

Venus's glyph resembles Mercury's, except for the half-circle on top and the symbol representing the female gender.

Positive Side

Venus makes us peaceful, loving, flirty, sensual, and elegant individuals. It also provides harmony and diplomacy during conflicts. This planet is typically associated with love, beauty, indulgence, expensive tastes, and luxury. Venus is the muse of art and culture and the personification of love itself. It also commands relationships, creativity, self-value, and how you receive love and affection. The iconic planet also influences your sense of fashion and personal style.

Negative Side

Venus can make us vain, self-centered, and self-indulgent. When Venus retrogrades, you may find yourself tempted to drastically change your physical appearance, wanting to get Botox shots, a nose job, or any form of cosmetic surgery.

Meaning

Venus is named after the Roman Goddess of love and beauty, Venus.

Mars

Glyph: ♂

The symbol of Mars is that of the male gender, and it represents the energy Mars provides you.

Positive Side

Aside from boosting your energy, Mars's presence in your zodiac sign makes you adventurous, driven, and assertive. Mars gives you the fire and passion to compete for your dream job or finish an important project on time. Simply put, it pushes you to move forward and achieve your goals.

Negative Side

Mars can make us rash, aggressive, and impulsive. When it retrogrades, it can lessen your sexual libido and makes you unable to defend or stand up for yourself.

Meaning

Mars is named after the Roman God of war, Mars. It represents passion, lust, and physical attraction. Where Venus represents love and emotions, Mars governs our sexual desires and most primal urges.

Jupiter

Glyph: ♃

Jupiter's symbol is a cross with a half-circle or crescent attached to it, representing our growth path until we eventually understand the meaning of life.

Positive Side

Jupiter's presence makes us optimistic, adventurous, positive, and compassionate. It provides us with a sense of humor and the ability to grow spiritually and mentally. This planet carries positive vibes that you will feel when it is present in your zodiac sign, bringing plenty of great opportunities with it. It is also associated with philosophy and education and broadens your mind. Jupiter motivates you to work hard to make your dreams come true. Whatever makes you happiest and most excited, Jupiter will push you to chase it.

Negative Side

The negative side of Jupiter includes bitterness, irresponsibility, overindulgence, and blind optimism.

Meaning

Jupiter is larger than all the other planets in our solar system. It is named after the Roman God of the sky, Jupiter, a symbol of luck, spirituality, and generosity.

Saturn

Glyph: ♄

Saturn's symbol is a cross with a half circle attached to its right side. It symbolizes how the planet helps us become aware of life's saddest yet truest realities, whether it's misery, old age, death, or decay. Once we fully understand and accept these realities, we can begin to grow.

Positive Side

Saturn's presence in the zodiac makes us resilient, disciplined, mature, and hard-working. It helps us achieve our professional goals and provides order, structure, and self-control to our lives. This planet wants to teach us lessons about overcoming our toughest challenges and help us grow, despite its apparent tough love. It is like a strict parent who wants the best for us but has unusual methods and lacks emotions.

Negative Side

Saturn teaches us lessons through challenges and hardships. When it retrogrades, we find ourselves restricted, and we may need to exert more effort to work or study.

Meaning

Saturn is named after the Roman God of agriculture, Saturn (or Saturnus). The planet represents time and boundaries.

Uranus

Glyph: ♅

Uranus's symbol is a cross representing matter, a circle at the bottom representing the spirit, and two half circles on either side, which symbolizes openness.

Positive Side

This planet governs creativity, objectivity, enlightenment, and progress. Uranus is unpredictable and full of surprises, and you can never know what it has in store since it is all about sudden changes. The planet not only influences individuals but also impacts the whole world through technology and revolutions. We should be grateful for Uranus as it makes life interesting and different.

Negative Side

Uranus can make you irresponsible and stir feelings of rebellion.

Meaning

Unlike other planets mentioned, Uranus is one of the few planets named after a Greek deity, not a Roman one. It is named after Uranus, the god of the sky. Where Saturn is about following the rules, Uranus is about breaking them and challenging the norm. Old isn't gold when it comes to Uranus as it is more concerned with innovation and forward-thinking. It doesn't care for traditions and wants what is new and unique.

Neptune

Glyph: ♆

Since Neptune is named after the God of the sea, it makes sense that its symbol is a trident. The cross represents matter, while the crescent represents openness.

Positive Side

The planet Neptune commands mercy, creativity, intuition, compassion, psychic power, and spiritual enlightenment.

Negative Side

Neptune can negatively impact our lives by stirring feelings of deceit, addiction, guilt, and delusion. Although it provides escapism that helps you deal with the difficulties of the real world, this planet can make you feel disconnected from reality. So, whenever you navigate your imagination, make sure you don't get lost.

Meaning

Neptune is named after the Roman god of the sea. Its mysticism is associated with illusion, dreams, fantasy, magic, the spirit, and intuition.

Pluto

Glyph: ♇

Last but not least is Pluto, which has two glyphs. The first one combines the initials of the person who discovered the planet: Percival Lowell. The "P" and the "L" are joined together to create the glyph. The second glyph is a crescent (spirit) and a cross (openness).

Positive Side

Pluto represents rebirth, growth, power, and new beginnings. This planet is associated with the transformation between two extremes, like day and night, ending and beginnings, etc. However, for this transformation to occur, you must let go of the past.

Negative Side

Pluto can be associated with negative patterns of behavior that include destruction, control, and a thirst for power.

Meaning

Pluto is named after the Roman God of the underworld, Pluto. Since it is the last planet in the solar system and is positioned furthest away from Earth, it has more of a collective than an individual impact on us.

Chapter 3: Analyzing Your Birth Chart

Fully grasping the art and science behind astrology is nearly impossible without taking the time to understand how to read a birth chart. Your sun sign is only part of the story, and the day on which an individual was born contains many other secrets that should be unlocked so you can better understand yourself and your trajectory. Astrology is a significant pathway to understand the world, but it must be employed to its fullest. Otherwise, it can only provide a piecemeal look at your life and those around you. This chapter will help clear up common misunderstandings regarding the birth chart and its use, so read on for more information about this complex and enigmatic aspect of astrology.

Creating a Birth Chart

Instead of visiting a professional astrologer, you can learn to create your birth chart. After all, the meat of this book is about making the work of astrology accessible to the largest audience possible, and creating a basic overview of tracking birth charts is not quite as complicated as it sounds.

To cast your birth chart, you will need a few pieces of vital yet easily accessible data: the time, date, and location of your birth. Perhaps the hardest bit of information to find might be the exact timing of your birth. Our parents tell us rather vague stories of when and how we were born - "it was late at night in the middle of a snowstorm," "my water broke at 2 PM, and then I was in labor for twelve hours," etc. The memories of stressed parents going into labor can't exactly be trusted, even if it's ostensibly the most memorable day of their lives. Suppose you need the precise time, but it does not appear on your birth certificate. In that case, there's a fairly simple workaround: call the local Vital Records office in your state and ask. If there's no record - which may very well be the case for those of us born in the early 1980s or earlier - then just make an estimate based on your family lore, or note 12 PM.

While we try to avoid estimates when it comes to the timing of your birth, it's still helpful to eyeball things. This is because, without this bit of information, you won't be able to know what your rising sign is, sometimes referred to as the ascendant. Also, you won't be able to properly assess the houses under which the planets in your chart fall, which is important data for you to know. At the same time, even a semi-accurate estimate will be enough since you will have your date and place of birth to rely on.

Once you have this information written down, you will have created a draft of the birth chart. Then, the next step is to compare it to the moving planets in the sky and their current positions. While this may be a rather heady endeavor at first, without the help of a professional astrologer, you can do your best to *guesstimate* by being creative. You can sketch out the inner wheel with blue planetary symbols since this is the fixed part of your birth chart that never changes. Next, draw out the outer wheel, which is the transitioning planets on the day you are creating the chart. Use the color orange, typically ascribed to this part of the chart. What follows will provide a detailed explanation of the different elements of a birth chart to help you properly identify them.

What Is the Ascendant?

On the day you were born, the planets were in the midst of their own planetary movements, telling a story separate from your own entirely, but which ultimately shapes you and reveals something about you. These movements, in turn, generate a sort of cosmic energy and a specific theme that influences your personality. So, the birth chart on the day you were born should tell you what the planets want to accomplish through you, while there are twelve different areas (or houses) in which these ideas are communicated. The ascendant placement ends up determining the entire system of houses in the birth chart. In short, the ascendant is a marker of your social personality and how people view you in light of your zodiac sign - it impacts your physical self and even your personal style.

Sun Sign

Whenever someone asks you about your astrological sign, they usually refer to your sun sign. Of course, there are twelve signs (Aries, Taurus, Pisces, Aquarius, Leo, Cancer, etc.). The sun sign is meant to denote your central identity and is the best expression of your true self. Once you have a date of birth, you can derive the associated sun sign. Once you have your sun sign, you can determine which of the four elements you belong to: air, water, fire, or earth. The four main elements drive the astrological sun signs, and they are essentially your truest self.

Moon Sign

Of course, the sun sign and the rising sign tell part of the story. To help you grasp the full picture, the moon sign is essential in letting you know the deep soul that lies behind your front-facing, socially acceptable identity. It is the subconscious side of your personality that is usually hidden from view but, at the same time, is the driving force behind your emotions. The moon sign can only be determined when you use the exact year of your birth, but once you know it, you'll be able to tell what drives your happiness, sadness, or pain. It also provides powerful insights into how you can nurture yourself or feel restored, so if you're looking for different self-care rituals that will help you, knowing the moon sign is crucial.

Identifying Your House Signs

Unlocking the mystery of your zodiac hinges on your capacity to identify the house signs properly. While the sun, moon, and rising signs are all crucial, you will now need a bit more information. In the same way, you have twelve signs to identify with; twelve houses can overlap with them. Each house represents an important marker in your life, from love to career, and each planet within the chart is located in both the sign and house. How they are placed can tremendously impact your life trajectory, so making sense of them is so useful. This, precisely, is where the work that goes into creating and deciphering a birth chart can become rather complex without the assistance of an astrologer. However, many clues can help you better understand your life story on your own.

Since the work can be demanding, treat it as a creative endeavor you can pursue in your downtime. As you sketch out the different elements, you can envision the houses and the signs like characters in a short story you're writing, each with their own unique personality quirks and certain aesthetic flourishes. Each of the planets expresses themselves in a style that is in sync with the sign where they reside, so think of the different character traits this way.

If this work becomes a bit unwieldy, there are free online birth chart generators you can play with, and you can simply input the necessary information. You may be provided with transit charts, which can tell you how to plan different things on your bucket list, whether it's a career change or moving to a new city. The planetary chart will simply tell you what has happened in your past, and you can probably even locate big milestones in your life thanks to the chart.

How to Identify the Planets

Astrology is deeply connected to the solar system, which helps inform this ancient practice. A full reading of your birth chart can be a serious challenge without fully understanding how to identify the planets. To boil it down, the birth chart is like a screenshot of the sky at the particular moment of your birth. It should help depict the exact location of each of the planets and the constellation they occupied when you were born. Seemingly insignificant details, such as the distance between the planets at that specific moment in time, are actually incredibly telling since they will reveal what the stars and planets were trying to communicate through you on that day.

Mercury is the planet of communication, reflecting logic and clarity. Quite the opposite of the moon sign, which drives your emotions. It governs the air signs of Gemini and Virgo, both of which represent fairly different elements. And, because Mercury takes roughly fourteen days to transit to another astrological sign, it goes into retrograde. This is where the famous fear of Mercury going into retrograde comes from - all communication is disrupted, and things go haywire.

Next, you have Venus, the planet that represents beauty and love. It rules over Taurus and Libra, and the romantic sensibilities can sometimes lead to bad decisions. This is why it's important to know when Venus goes retrograde since it may induce major life-changing decisions that people immediately regret.

Mars is an impulsive planet, and it rules over Aries. People who suddenly feel a fire in their belly and are ruled by their passions tend to fall under the spell of this planet. Then there's Jupiter, in charge of philosophy and fortune. It governs Sagittarius, which is known for its fiery yet deeply thoughtful nature.

Saturn represents hard work, and it makes sense that it would govern Capricorn. It's the sign that fosters tough love and ambition, so it tends to command all career-related aspects in someone's life. Uranus governs Aquarius, and it's the planet that drives rebellion and innovation.

For those interested in the unknown and understanding spirituality, the planet Neptune and its position in your birth chart are paramount. It's the sign that governs Pisces, and when it's fully present, it tends to enhance one's intuition. The planet associated with power and domination is Pluto, and as such, it governs Scorpio.

Significance of Placement on the Birth Chart

The importance of planets and their relationship to the zodiac allows you to understand your journey to the stars. The planets listed above directly impact our personalities and how we experience daily life. You will have an inner and outer chart, and each of these charts is further divided into twelve houses. Each house in your chart represents a specific aspect of your life. These houses cover everything from how you manage finances and relationships to the smaller aspects of your character. When you are in tune with each of these houses, you can better understand why you act certain ways in situations and use that to your advantage. This will help you to better plan for the future and develop yourself around your core beliefs, characteristics, and philosophies. You can also delve into your weaknesses and use your strengths to balance them.

Astrology is a complex and intricate study, to say the least. It is not simply a "woo-woo" style of New Age-y, hipster-driven concepts that people do for fun. Yes, it can be enjoyable to talk about sun signs and moon signs, but a full appreciation of the astrological alignment at the specific time of your birth can be quite an illuminating experience. The birth chart, when done well, can help you understand the areas in your life that are going well - so that you don't self-sabotage - as well as those that require improvement so that you can grow as an individual and carve your own path towards spiritual emancipation.

Chapter 4: The Twelve Zodiac Signs

This is the part you have been waiting for! This dedicated chapter will delve into the most popular and interesting part of astrology, zodiac signs. After having explained what zodiac signs are in the first part of the book, we will now discuss each one in detail.

Aries

Ruling Planet

Mars

Meaning

Ram

Element

Fire

Qualities

Aries are brave, courageous, ambitious, honest, confident, self-assertive, and bold individuals. They are known to be fearless and risk-takers. They never turn down new experiences, no matter how crazy or out there. Your Aries friend is the perfect person to call if you want someone to climb a mountain or go skydiving with you. They are also creative, passionate, optimistic, generous, and filled with energy. An Aries always looks forward to the future and leaves the past behind. Need help? Call an Aries as they never hesitate about lending a helping hand.

Aries have a few negative qualities as well. They can exhibit a bad temper, and it can take them a while before they can calm down. They can be guilty of blind optimism and jumping headfirst without considering the consequences. While a little competitiveness doesn't hurt, Aries can be too competitive at times. They can also be reckless, selfish, attention seekers, and impatient.

Aries are intelligent and natural-born leaders, which makes them perfect for management positions.

Opposite Sign

Libra

Mantra

Patience, patience!

The Most Compatible Signs

Gemini, Leo, and Libra

The Least Compatible Signs

Taurus, Cancer, and Aries

Taurus

Ruling Planet

Venus

Meaning

Bull

Element

Earth

Qualities

Tauruses are reliable, and you can depend on them for anything. They are stable, persistent, and consistent individuals. They are happy and comfortable with the status quo and aren't fans of changes or shake-ups. It isn't a good idea to try and take a Taurus out of their comfort zone or make them feel unsafe; otherwise, they will turn green with rage, like the Hulk. Tauruses are honest people who don't like being lied to. They are incredibly hard-working, focused, and ambitious. Combine this with their reliability, and you will have yourself the perfect employee. Taurus's work hard to afford the finer things in life, as they have expensive tastes and enjoy spoiling themselves.

In parallel, Taurus's are stubborn, resistant to change, and would challenge anyone they believe is wrong, even authority figures like their boss. During long breaks, Taurus's may enjoy relaxation a little too much and end up feeling lazy and start to procrastinate. They are perfectionists and won't accept anything less than the high standard they have set for themselves.

Opposite Sign

Scorpio

Mantra

Embrace change!

The Most Compatible Signs

Virgo, Capricorn, and Scorpio

The Least Compatible Signs

Leo and Aquarius

Gemini

Ruling Planet

Mercury

Meaning

Twins

Elements

Air

Qualities

Geminis are renowned for being easy-going and are the kind of people who would never say no to trying new things. They are extremely flexible and enjoy having fun and going on adventures. Unlike Taurus, the Gemini is adaptable to change. They are social butterflies, and if you meet a Gemini at a party, strike up a conversation with them. They are chatty and have interesting stories to share. This is mainly because Geminis are clever, intellectual, and enjoy reading, which makes them distinguished conversationalists.

By contrast, Geminis struggle with making decisions because of their need to analyze everything. However, on occasion, they can be guilty of making reckless decisions and being impulsive. For that reason, you can't rely on Geminis as they can be irresponsible and unable to commit to plans.

They are curious, passionate, and outspoken, which makes them excel in creative jobs like writer, artist, or journalist.

Opposite Sign

Sagittarius

Mantra

Hit the pause button!

The Most Compatible Signs

Libra, Aquarius, and Sagittarius

Cancer

Ruling Planet

The Moon

Meaning

Crab

Element

Water

Qualities

Cancers are one of the most loyal signs, but it will take time for them to trust you fully. They are extremely devoted and will turn mountains for the people they love. If you have a Cancer friend or relative, consider yourself lucky. Cancers would go above and beyond to protect the people in their lives. They are empathetic, intuitive, and emotionally intelligent, which gives them the ability to read people. Cancers are also notoriously caring, loving, and kind.

Cancers don't handle criticism well due to their over-sensitive nature. Since their planet is the moon, Cancer's emotions are like the tide, sometimes high and sometimes low. If you cross them, people under this sign can be petty and manipulative, especially when they don't get their way.

Cancers are creative, adaptable, and organized and prefer secure jobs with steady pay.

Opposite Sign

Capricorn

Mantra

Own it!

The Most Compatible Signs

Pisces, Scorpio, and Capricorn

The Least Compatible Signs

Gemini, Libra, Aquarius, Leo, Aries, and Sagittarius

Leo

Ruling Planet

The Sun

Meaning

Lion

Element

Fire

Qualities

Leos are known to be very confident, which makes sense since the king of the jungle is their symbol. They are commanding, powerful, and unapologetic. They are not only confident in their abilities but in their loved ones as well, which is why your Leo friend will always cheer you on and believe in you more than anyone. They are extremely generous, not just with money but with their time, love, and affection as well. Determined and optimistic, Leos can achieve any goal they set their mind to. Leos are also charismatic, which makes them ideal for leadership and community-building roles.

Some Leos are often guilty of arrogance and having disproportionate egos. They can also be stubborn, especially when they have a goal to achieve. Rather than ask for help or try to imagine new ways to achieve their goals, they prefer to stick to what they know. Leos don't handle criticism very well due to their high self-confidence and think they are above criticism because they do everything right.

Opposite Sign

Aquarius

Mantra

It is ok to just *be...*

The Most Compatible Signs

Aries, Leo, Sagittarius, Libras, and Aquarius

The Least Compatible Signs

Cancer, Pisces, Scorpio, Taurus, Capricorn, and Virgo

Virgo

Ruling Planet

Mercury

Meaning

Maiden or virgin

Element

Earth

Qualities

Virgos are creative individuals who enjoy artistic activities. They are extremely hard-working and don't rest until they get the job done. They are considered one of the most responsible signs in the zodiac and excel when they are in charge. Virgos are patient with the people in their lives and can give them more than one chance. They never hesitate to lend a helping hand, thanks to their kind and benevolent nature.

By contrast, Virgos can be stubborn and think they are always right. People born under this sign set high standards for themselves and everyone around them and can get overly critical if someone doesn't meet these standards. They are also known for being overthinkers and inflexible.

Opposite Sign

Pisces

Mantra

Imperfection is beautiful.

The Most Compatible Signs

Taurus, Capricorn, Scorpio, and Cancer

The Least Compatible Signs

Libra and Aquarius

Libra

Ruling Planet

Venus

Meaning

Scales

Element

Air

Qualities

Libras are known for being diplomatic individuals who always manage to keep the peace. This is because they know what to say, what not to say, and how to compromise. With the scales as their symbol, Libras strive for justice and balance. They are also highly extroverted and considered social butterflies. Libras are great at making new friends thanks to their innate social nature and love to be around people.

The glass is always full in Libras' view. Whether it is with people, at work, or in the household, they see the best in everything and everyone. If you have a problem, reach out to your Libra friend. They are smart and witty people with vivid imaginations who can easily find a solution to any problem.

Libras have trouble making decisions, whether big or small. A Libra will spend hours analyzing all outcomes before making up their mind. Because they appreciate the beauty and the finer things in life, they can be vain and overly concerned with their physical appearance. As a result of their peaceful nature, Libras struggle with confrontations, whether it is with people or problems.

Opposite Sign

Aries

Mantra

Speak my mind.

The Most Compatible Signs

Aquarius, Gemini, Libra, and Aries

The Least Compatible Signs

Scorpio, Cancer, Pisces, Virgo, Taurus, and Capricorns

Scorpio

Ruling Planets

Mars and Pluto

Meaning

Scorpion

Element

Water

Qualities

Scorpio's courage knows no boundaries. They are the first people to jump into a burning building to save others. Scorpios are focused, and when they set their mind to something, they can become unstoppable. They are determined, focused, and ambitious individuals. The word impossible doesn't exist in their dictionary. They are loyal, honest, and very dedicated in their relationships.

You can never control a Scorpion, although they can easily control you and any situation because they believe they know what's best. They treat everything in life as a competition which can make them prone to jealousy, especially when someone excels in a certain domain. This can also make them hold grudges and even become resentful. Scorpions are very secretive even with their emotions, which can frustrate the people in their lives.

Opposite Sign

Taurus

Mantra

Don't hide!

The Most Compatible Signs

Cancer, Pisces, Scorpios, and Taurus

The Least Compatible Signs

Libra, Aquarius, Gemini

Sagittarius

Ruling Planet

Jupiter

Meaning

Archer

Element

Fire

Qualities

Sagittarius is considered the most independent zodiac sign. They love being free to chase their goals and dreams. No one can see the bigger picture more than a Sagittarius, which makes them the right people from which to seek advice. They can befriend anyone thanks to their empathetic, compassionate, and warm nature. They genuinely care about others and accept them for who they are. Sagittarius hate deception and dishonesty because they are honest, trustworthy, and straightforward individuals.

Owing to their independent nature, Sagittarius's are not always team players and tend to clash with the concept of authority. Their ego can sometimes get the best of them and render them unable to handle criticism. Sagittarius's tend to think that others are as well-intentioned as they are, which can lead to disappointments and being taken advantage of. They don't know how to draw the line between honesty and being hurtful. In other words, they will tell you what they think without consideration for your feelings.

Opposite Sign

Gemini

Mantra

Focus and Commit!

The Most Compatible Signs

Aries, Leo, Sagittarius, Libra, Aquarius, and Gemini

The Least Compatible Signs

Virgo, Taurus, and Capricorn

Capricorn

Ruling Planet

Saturn

Meaning

Goat

Element

Earth

Qualities

Capricorns are very responsible and mature individuals. They are organized, law-abiding, and aren't afraid to admit when they are wrong. In fact, no sign in the zodiac is as serious as Capricorns. They are persistent individuals who never give up until they get what they want. People born under this sign love learning new things and constantly working on bettering themselves.

Because of their ambition and desire to be on top, Capricorns can be workaholics and refuse to take a break until they achieve their goals. This can lead to exhaustion and stress. They can take life too seriously, which can prevent them from seeing the bright side. Their glass is always half empty, making them miserable. They are perfectionists, and if anything isn't up to their standard, they can be quite disappointed. Getting along with a Capricorn can be difficult because of their stubbornness and inability to see things from other people's perspectives.

Opposite Sign

Cancer

Mantra

I don't need to do it all!

The Most Compatible Signs

Capricorn, Virgo, Taurus, Pisces, Scorpion, and Cancer

The Least Compatible Signs

Libra, Gemini, and Aquarius

Aquarius

Ruling Planets

Saturn and Uranus

Meaning

Water-bearer

Element

Air

Qualities

Aquarians are compassionate individuals who are born to make the world a better place. They are the first people to volunteer for a humanitarian cause. Those born under this sign stand out from the crowd because they are unique and happy to embrace their quirkiness. The word "ordinary" doesn't exist in their dictionary. They are creative people with out-of-the-box ideas. If you are wondering about how quirky an Aquarius can be, just think of Phoebe Buffay from the TV show Friends. They are intelligent and analytical people who are tolerant of ideas different from their own.

With their intelligence, Aquarians see themselves as being always right, discarding other people's opinions as invalid without a second thought. This can lead them to talk down to others without realizing it. Since they are over-analyzers, Aquarians can put their feelings aside and deal with things pragmatically, which can make them come across as cold and emotionally detached. However, they will sometimes express their emotions in the form of unpredictable anger outbursts. Aquarians have an idealistic vision of what the world should be rather than what it really is. This can make them feel unsatisfied, hopeless, and depressed.

Opposite Sign

Leo

Mantra

My uniqueness is my gift!

The Most Compatible Signs

Libra, Gemini, Aquarius, Sagittarius, Aries, and Leo

The Least Compatible Signs

Cancer, Scorpio, Pisces

Pisces

Ruling Planets

Neptune and Jupiter

Meaning

Fish

Element

Water

Qualities

Last but definitely not least, Pisces deeply care about other people in their lives. They are generous and would do anything to make their loved ones happy. They are imaginative and creative individuals who express their creativity through various art forms. Pisces is the friend everyone needs. They are great listeners, and you will never find someone more empathetic and emotionally understanding than a Pisces. They are kind and sweet and would do anything to make you feel better whenever they sense sadness or despair.

That said, Pisces's own emotions can sometimes get out of hand. During a heated conversation, a Pisces may shut down. They don't recover easily once their mood is altered and may even hold grudges. Pisces are often taken advantage of because of their generous nature, which can hurt their feelings and disappoint them. As a defense mechanism, Pisces would build a wall around themselves for protection. Pisces aren't the most logical thinkers, and for that reason, they tend to have unrealistic goals or dreams.

Opposite Sign

Virgo

Mantra

I trust what the universe will bring my way.

Most Compatible Signs

Taurus, Scorpio, Pisces, Virgo, Cancer, and Capricorn

Least Compatible Signs

Leo, Gemini, Libra, Sagittarius, Aquarius, and Aries

Chapter 5: Astrological Divination

Astrological divination observes the planets and the stars. This includes all heavenly bodies in our solar system, the sun, and moon – along with the many stars in multiple other solar systems. The planets are studied to help us see into the future of our own lives.

Believers in astrological divination hold that knowing how the stars and planets can impact worldly matters allows them to forecast and alter the fates of people, communities, and states. Many societies, such as Indian, Chinese, and Western in general, have valued astrological divination for ages and have built formal systems for forecasting earthly events based on in-depth planetary studies.

This chapter will review several kinds of important astrological divination, with a particular focus on Western practice. Without further ado, let's get started.

Interpretation of Birth Charts to Forecast Human Events

Perhaps the most common type of astrology in the West is the interpretation of birth charts. It is all about explaining different parts of a person's character and predicting significant future events in their lives. These birth chart interpretations involve observing and analyzing the planetary movements, the sun, and the moon pertaining to the time of their birth.

In Indian, Chinese, and Western cultures, an astrological forecast or divination for an activity is predicated based on the unique planetary position of the sun, moon, and stars at the time of the occurrence. In astrology, each event is crucial. Since there is a significantly strong relationship between someone's time of birth and the attributes ingrained in their character, an astrologer can unearth fundamental insights about that person simply by looking at the moment of their birth.

Astrologers examine birth charts to learn about someone's patterns of life events, talents, potential, strengths, weaknesses, and internal strife. These interpretations can help guide people's decisions when they choose to consult an astrologer.

You can also interpret your own birth chart by learning some of the fundamentals astrologers use to interpret these charts. To that end, you need to know about the various meanings of astrological signs, houses, and planets. To interpret your birth chart, use the following formula:

Sign + Planet + House = Interpretation

Sign Interpretation

When interpreting your birth chart, look to the outer section that is split into 12 parts. One of those areas will contain your name and date of birth. This is the part that determines your Astrological sign. The

Astrological chart features 12 signs, each representing a singular character quality.

Your Astrological sign can influence your personality to a great extent. For instance, if you're an Aries, you're said to be enthusiastic, motivated, somehow aggressive, and extroverted. You may learn more about the prominent astrological personality features online or purchase an astrological guidebook from your local bookstore. If you're lucky, you can even borrow one from a friend or find it at your municipal library,

Remember that your Astrological sign is only one factor in interpreting a birth chart and that several other factors do influence the way your sign is interpreted. To fully understand the astrological analysis of a birth chart and grasp its significance, you must examine the other components of the chart, such as your houses and planetary arrangements. This information is essentially based on your exact time and place of birth.

Interpretation of Houses

To figure out how the houses in your birth chart will be designated, you'll first need to identify the ascendant. As a crucial component, a birth chart's ascendant refers to the precise position on the Eastern horizon at the time of your birth, as measured by signs and degrees.

If your astrological chart or birth chart is like a clock, then your ascendant would be at nine o'clock. As you know, a birth chart is divided into 12 inner divisions. Starting from the ascendant, you can count your first house counterclockwise. In a birth chart, there are 12 houses. These houses represent various parts of your life events.

- The first house represents your identity, physical features, personality, character, and other natural characteristics.

- The second house represents your wealth, financial belongings, and "money" mindset.

- The third house represents communication and travel. It governs how people communicate with you, as well as tangible ways of communicating such as mail and short journeys.

- The fourth house represents our household, relatives, and possessions. This house defines your origins, history, upbringing, and the inner feelings that come from these aspects of your lifestyle.

- The fifth house represents your kids or offspring and how you interact with them.

- The sixth house represents health during your lifetime.

- The seventh house is associated with committed, long-term relations. This house has authority over matrimony and romantic relationships. It demonstrates what you are looking for in a long-term companion.

- The eighth house represents regeneration and rejuvenation.

- The ninth house represents your physical and emotional traveling, which has a great impact on your life.

- The tenth house represents your career and professional aspirations. It is where you'll find your dreams and goals.

- The eleventh house represents your sense of hope and your accomplished dreams.

- Lastly, the twelfth house represents your hidden secrets.

Interpretation of Planetary Movements

The planets that pass through various houses in your birth chart impact your interpretation. Planets are depicted by various characters across the chart. Their rotation can unleash forces that can influence your everyday life, personally, socially, professionally, and spiritually.

A circle with just a mark in the center represents the sun. The moon is shaped like a half-crescent. The feminine sign is Venus, whereas the masculine sign is Mars. The feminine sign is Mercury, with two little lines sticking out of the upper circle. Jupiter is symbolized by a sign that resembles the number four. Saturn is symbolized by a sign that looks like a 5. Uranus, Neptune, and Pluto are all represented by more complex symbols. Uranus resembles a flipside feminine sign, with two arcs on each side. Neptune resembles a flipside cross with two upwards spiraling lines along both sides. Pluto is a planet that resembles a cross between Neptune and Uranus. It's a feminine sign looking upright, with two looping lines along both sides.

In astrological interpretation, there are two main kinds of planets: Personal planets and outer planets. The personal planets are Mercury, Mars, Venus, the sun, and the moon. All remaining planets are outer planets.

The sun symbolizes a person's life purpose and meaning. The moon represents a person's reaction to and reflection on their own life experiences. Mercury governs your capacity to comprehend people and connect with them meaningfully. Venus represents your comfort zone. Mars is the planet that symbolizes your willpower and deeds.

The great Jupiter governs your social integration and inner development. Saturn is the planet that symbolizes your duties and the individual regulations you build through time. Uranus commands all learning and growth. Neptune is the planet of ideas and creativity. Lastly, Pluto shows your ability for evolution and intimate changes.

To understand yours correctly, you must evaluate where the planets reside in a birth chart. What house are they in, and what sign are they holding? This will provide you with information about your life and personal character. Planets reflect what you do for a living or what motivates you, and houses indicate your approach to completing a particular activity. As for the signs, they indicate where you might anticipate certain characteristics of development or progress in your life.

Why Is It Important?

Invariably, our lives are in rhythm due to unexpected events that take place when you least expect them. It might be a roller coaster ride of joyous feelings, followed by episodes of anguish and despair.

Although you cannot change the past, you can, to some extent, influence what happens in the future. This is where astrological divination comes into perspective because it helps you create a knowledgeable vision of your future. There is a possibility you may find a route out of your day-to-day worries and concerns thanks to astrology, and it can only be predicted through planetary cycles and birth charts.

Astrology has helped and continues to help millions of people all around the world since its inception. For that reason alone, predicting planetary cycles and birth charts is more valuable than you would think. This practice can also help you figure out what vocation is best suited and will provide you with the most happiness and gratification. This means that, instead of wasting time here and there, you can focus on honing the talents and abilities your ideal job will require. Moreover, a birth chart can reveal how a person's love life will evolve, which sign they are most compatible with, and how happy their relationship will be overall. It helps you understand the ifs and buts that may arise in a relationship.

What's great about astrological divination is it does not discriminate based on age, gender, or social status. It enables everybody to transition from an insecure existence to a safe, more rewarding one. In a nutshell, your birth charts can help you become more confident about your life, thanks to astrological predictions.

Regardless of what your goal may be, astrological divination and interpreting your birth chart enables you to understand the unique signs, houses, and planetary arrangements that are unique to your time and place of birth. While you may have to spend a lot of time analyzing your birth chart at first, practice and dedication will empower you with great insights into your own life and how to take charge of it. Do not shy away from creating dynamic narratives and making out-of-the-box observations. Your innate curiosity will be the one thing illuminating the darkness.

Conclusion

The stars up above not only light up the skies but also serve as maps to help guide us through our lives. Astrology is a complex and fascinating subject. It shows us the universe has a plan for us and that this plan has been in motion since the day we were born. We are connected to the universe around us, and everything that happens in the skies can affect our lives, one way or another. This is what makes astrology so fascinating and interesting to study.

We opened this book with a simple Astrology 101 explaining its origins, branches, and practice. We also explained popular terms that you may not be familiar with, like horoscopes, zodiac signs, and birth charts. We then discussed the planets and how their positioning can affect our personality, whether on a daily basis like with "inner planets" or impact generations or societies like "outer planets."

Also discussed at length were birth charts and how they act as maps of our lives and future. We talked about what these charts can reveal about your personality and certain events in your life. If you remember, a birth chart allows you to identify your zodiac sign, zodiac house, ascendant sun sign, moon sign, and other information that will provide insight into your personality.

We then delved into zodiac signs and provided all the information about each one, including the qualities and flaws inherent to each sign. We dedicated the last portion to astrological predictions, how astrologers interpret birth charts and the movements of the planets, so they can predict the future of individuals and events that can impact the whole planet.

Now that you have familiarized yourself with the fundamentals of astrology, you can begin to use the concept you learned to gain a deeper understanding of yourself and the people in your life and predict your future!

Here's another book by Silvia Hill that you might like

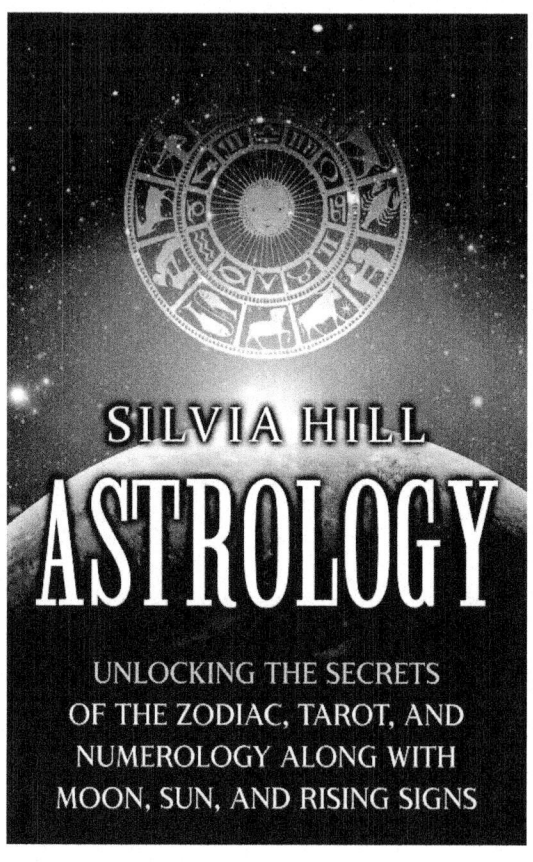

Free Bonus from Silvia Hill
available for limited time

Hi Spirituality Lovers!

My name is Silvia Hill, and first off, I want to THANK YOU for reading my book.

Now you have a chance to join my exclusive spirituality email list so you can get the ebooks below for free as well as the potential to get more spirituality ebooks for free! Simply click the link below to join.

P.S. Remember that it's 100% free to join the list.

~~$27~~ FREE BONUSES

- ❤️ 9 Types of Spirit Guides and How to Connect to Them
- ❤️ How to Develop Your Intuition: 7 Secrets for Psychic Development and Tarot Reading
- ❤️ Tarot Reading Secrets for Love, Career, and General Messages

Access your free bonuses here
https://livetolearn.lpages.co/silvia-astrology-for-beginners/

References

Flanagan, R. (n.d.). *Riley's astrology corner: How astrology can change your life*. The Spectator. https://seattlespectator.com/2021/04/28/rileys-astrology-corner-how-astrology-can-change-your-life

Guest Column. (n.d.). *5 reasons to study astrology and how it can help your personal growth*. Smudailycampus.Com. https://www.smudailycampus.com/sponsoredcontent/tactadv/5-reasons-to-study-astrology-and-how-it-can-help-your-personal-growth

Thomas, K. (2021, November 16). What is a birth chart in astrology — and how do you read one? *New York Post*. https://nypost.com/article/astrology-birth-chart

astrology - Astrology in modern times. (n.d.). In *Encyclopedia Britannica*.

Astrology Zodiac Signs. (n.d.). *Branches of astrology*. Astrology-Zodiac-Signs.Com. https://www.astrology-zodiac-signs.com/astrology/branches

History of astrology. (n.d.). Historyworld.Net. http://www.historyworld.net/wrldhis/plaintexthistories.asp?historyid=ac32

Kelly, A. (2018, March 12). *Birth charts 101: Understanding the planets and their meanings*. Allure. https://www.allure.com/story/astrology-birth-chart-reading

Stuckrad, K. von. (2016). Astrology. In *A Companion to Science, Technology, and Medicine in Ancient Greece and Rome* (pp. 114–129). John Wiley & Sons, Inc.

The Editors of Encyclopedia Britannica. (2008). horoscope. In *Encyclopedia Britannica*

The Editors of Encyclopedia Britannica. (2021). astrology summary. In *Encyclopedia Britannica.*

(N.d.). Time.Com. https://time.com/5315377/are-zodiac-signs-real-astrology-history

Camacho, N. A. (2022, April 9). *Personal and general planets affect you differently—here's what each means, according to astrologers.* Well+Good. https://www.wellandgood.com/personal-generational-planets

Coughlin, S. (2017, July 3). *Understanding how those mysterious outer planets affect your sign.* Refinery29. https://www.refinery29.com/en-us/2017/07/161612/outer-planet-solar-system-zodiac-sign-effect

DiCara, V. A. P. by. (2010, June 21). *Symbols and glyphs of astrology.* Vic DiCara's Astrology. https://vicdicara.wordpress.com/2010/06/21/symbols-and-glyphs-of-astrology

Jupiter, king of the gods, in Astrology/zodiac. (2015, April 13). Cafeastrology.Com. https://cafeastrology.com/jupiter.html

Kahn, N. (2019, January 28). *Your guide to the planets in astrology & how they affect you.* Bustle. https://www.bustle.com/life/how-each-planets-astrology-directly-affects-every-zodiac-sign-13098560

Kelly, A. (2018, March 12). *Birth charts 101: Understanding the planets and their meanings.* Allure. https://www.allure.com/story/astrology-birth-chart-reading

Mars, god of war, in Astrology/zodiac. (2015, April 13). Cafeastrology.Com. https://cafeastrology.com/mars.html

Neptune, god of the sea, in Astrology/zodiac. (2015, May 8). Cafeastrology.Com. https://cafeastrology.com/neptune.html

Planet types in astrology. (2020, October 24). Star World News. https://starworldnews.com/planet-types-in-astrology

Pluto. (2015, May 8). Cafeastrology.Com. https://cafeastrology.com/pluto.html

Role and importance of planets in astrology. (n.d.). Shrivinayakaastrology.Com. http://www.shrivinayakaastrology.com/Planets/roleofplanets.html

Saturn in Astrology, zodiac. (2015, April 19). Cafeastrology.Com. https://cafeastrology.com/saturn.html

Saturn (mythology). (n.d.). Newworldencyclopedia.Org. https://www.newworldencyclopedia.org/entry/Saturn_(mythology)

Scanlon, C. (2020, January 21). *The inner planets in astrology and their meaning.* Global Bizarre. https://globalbizarre.com/inner-planets-in-astrology

Sloan, E. (2021, July 13). *Here's what each planet actually means in astrology—so you can understand your chart in more depth.* Well+Good. https://www.wellandgood.com/meanings-of-planets-in-astrology

The Moon in Astrology/zodiac. (2015, May 11). Cafeastrology.Com. https://cafeastrology.com/moon.html

The Sun in Astrology, the zodiac. (2015, May 8). Cafeastrology.Com. https://cafeastrology.com/sun.html

Thomas, K. (2021, November 5). A guide to the planets in astrology and what they each represent. *New York Post.* https://nypost.com/article/astrology-planets-meaning

Uranus, god of the sky, in Astrology/zodiac. (2015, May 8). Cafeastrology.Com. https://cafeastrology.com/uranus.html

Venus, goddess of love, in Astrology. (2015, April 19). Cafeastrology.Com. https://cafeastrology.com/venus.html

WatsonContributor, E., & 03/16/, Z. (2021, March 16). *Outer planets in astrology: Effects & zodiac sign house meanings.* YourTango. https://www.yourtango.com/2021339762/outer-planets-astrology-effects-zodiac-sign-house-meanings

AstroTwins. What is an astrology birth chart? Your natal chart explained. Astrostyle: Astrology and Daily, Weekly, Monthly Horoscopes by The AstroTwins. Published August 26, 2016. https://astrostyle.com/astrology-birth-chart

Stardust L. How to create your own astrology birth chart. Vogue. Published March 26, 2021. https://www.vogue.com/article/how-to-create-your-own-astrology-birth-chart

Sloan E. Here's what each planet actually means in astrology—so you can understand your chart in more depth. Well+Good. Published July 13, 2021. https://www.wellandgood.com/meanings-of-planets-in-astrology

Kelly A. Birth charts 101: Understanding the planets and their meanings. Allure. Published March 12, 2018. https://www.allure.com/story/astrology-birth-chart-reading

Andriani, L. (2018, April 26). *The best mantra for your zodiac sign.* Oprah.Com. https://www.oprah.com/inspiration/best-mantra-for-your-zodiac-sign

Astrology, T. O. I. (2021, August 10). *Aries Personality Traits: Positive vs Negative you should be aware of.* Times Of India. https://timesofindia.indiatimes.com/astrology/zodiacs-astrology/traits/aries-personality-traits-positive-vs-negative-you-should-be-aware-of/articleshow/85204806.cms

Cabral, C. (n.d.-a). *The 10 fundamental Libra traits and the best advice for Libras.* Prepscholar.Com. https://blog.prepscholar.com/libra-traits-personality

Cabral, C. (n.d.-b). *The 10 key Virgo traits and the best advice for Virgos.* Prepscholar.Com. https://blog.prepscholar.com/virgo-traits-personality

Cabral, C. (n.d.-c). *The 10 Scorpio personality traits to know.* Prepscholar.Com. https://blog.prepscholar.com/scorpio-personality-traits

Douglas, M. (n.d.). *The fundamental 6 Pisces traits, explained.* Prepscholar.Com. https://blog.prepscholar.com/pisces-traits

Kelly, A. (2018, February 2). *The personality of an Aries, explained.* Allure. https://www.allure.com/story/aries-zodiac-sign-personality-traits

King, K. (2021, May 4). *What's your opposite sign in astrology - and what does it mean?* Metro.Co.Uk. https://metro.co.uk/2021/05/04/whats-your-opposite-sign-in-astrology-and-what-does-it-mean-14518677

Logan, B. (n.d.-a). *The 8 Aries traits you need to know.* Prepscholar.Com https://blog.prepscholar.com/aries-traits-personality

Logan, B. (n.d.-b). *The 8 fundamental Taurus traits, explained.* Prepscholar.Com. https://blog.prepscholar.com/taurus-traits-personality

Muniz, H. (n.d.-a). *The 6 fundamental Capricorn traits, explained.* Prepscholar.Com. https://blog.prepscholar.com/capricorn-traits-personality

Muniz, H. (n.d.-b). *The 7 Aquarius traits you need to know.* Prepscholar.Com. https://blog.prepscholar.com/aquarius-traits-personality

Muniz, H. (n.d.-c). *The 7 fundamental Cancer traits and what they mean for you.* Prepscholar.Com. https://blog.prepscholar.com/cancer-traits-personality

Norris, R. (2022, April 13). *3 signs that are completely compatible with Aries—and 3 that certainly Aren't.* Well+Good. https://www.wellandgood.com/who-is-aries-compatible-with

Regan, S. (2022c, February 7). *Leo compatibility: What to know about dating or befriending this sign.* Mindbodygreen. https://www.mindbodygreen.com/articles/leo-sign-101

Regan, S. (2022e, February 7). *Meet Gemini: The wise & witty air sign of the zodiac.* Mindbodygreen. https://www.mindbodygreen.com/articles/gemini-sign-101

Regan, S. (2022i, February 7). *This sign is the "boss" of the zodiac—but it's often misunderstood.* Mindbodygreen. https://www.mindbodygreen.com/articles/capricorn

Regan, S. (2022k, February 15). *Meet Pisces: The go-with-the-flow psychic of the zodiac.* Mindbodygreen. https://www.mindbodygreen.com/articles/pisces-sign-101

Robinson, A. (n.d.-a). *The 5 fundamental Sagittarius traits you need to know.* Prepscholar.Com. https://blog.prepscholar.com/sagittarius-traits-personality

Robinson, A. (n.d.-b). *The 8 key Leo traits: Your guide to the august zodiac sign.* Prepscholar.Com. https://blog.prepscholar.com/leo-traits-personality

RoseAuthor, K., & 08/22/, Z. (2020, August 22). *What does the Aries symbol & glyph mean?* YourTango.

https://www.yourtango.com/2020336399/aries-symbol-zodiac-sign-glyphs-meanings

Seigel, D. (n.d.). *The 7 fundamental Gemini traits, explained.* Prepscholar.Com. https://blog.prepscholar.com/gemini-traits

Sloan, E. (2021, August 19). *What exactly are the astrological elements? An astrologer shares their origins and meanings.* Well+Good. https://www.wellandgood.com/elements-astrological-signs

Printed in Dunstable, United Kingdom

72136520R00040